The Phoenix Living Poets

MEN WITHOUT EVENINGS

The Phoenix Living Poets

MEASURES
A ROUND OF APPLAUSE
A COMMON GRACE
Norman MacCaig
THIS COLD UNIVERSE
THE WORLD I SEE
Patric Dickinson
ADDICTIONS
SOME MEN ARE BROTHERS
THE OLD ADAM
D. J. Enright
WHEN THAT APRIL
Gillian Stoneham
POEMS
Lotte Zurndorfer
TIME FOR SALE
Edward Lowbury
SELECTED POEMS
James Merrill
THE SUN MY MONUMENT
Laurie Lee
FAIRGROUND MUSIC
John Fuller
THE RE-ORDERING OF THE STONES
NATURE WITH MAN
Jon Silkin
CONTROL TOWER
Richard Kell
THE SWANS OF BERWICK
Sydney Tremayne
WORDS FOR BLODWEN
Gloria Evans Davies
POEMS
Alexander Baird
THE DIRECTIONS OF MEMORY
Laurence Lerner
SELECTED POEMS
Robert Pack
THE YEAR OF THE WHALE
George Mackay Brown
THE BURNING HARE
J. C. Hall

MEN
WITHOUT EVENINGS

by

DAVID GILL

CHATTO AND WINDUS

THE HOGARTH PRESS

1966

Published by
Chatto and Windus Ltd
with The Hogarth Press Ltd
42 William IV Street
London WC2

★

Clarke, Irwin and Co Ltd
Toronto

Printed in Great Britain by
T. H. Brickell and Son Ltd
The Blackmore Press, Gillingham, Dorset

Contents

Men Without Evenings	page 9
Them	11
Them and Us	13
The Conservatives	14
The Kaleidoscope	15
Rendez-vous	16
Not needed	17
African Lovers	18
Tandem	19
Euphorbia Trees	20
Swamp	21
Trial	22
Big-game Hunter	23
The Expatriate	24
Perfect Beggar	25
Bakonjo	26
The Secessionists	27
The Mission	28
Political Prisoners	29
So we're All Right, Mum	30
Feud	31
On the Great Bitter Lakes	32
Vultures	33
A Non-elegy in a National Game Park	34
Dry Safari	35
Too Fragile	36
Murchison	37
Stuck	38
Wildebeests	39
Albert Nyanza	40
Ankole	40
Fulfilment	41
An Old Man Speaks . . .	41

Idyll	42
African Night	43
Co-existence	44
Fish	45
Independence Anniversary	46
Congolese Rebel	47
Evening Cigarette	48

Acknowledgements are due to the editors of the following periodicals and publications, in which some of the poems first appeared: *The Critical Quarterly, Delta, The Listener, P.E.N. New Poems* 1966, *Tribune.*

Men Without Evenings

(Was frommt's, dergleichen viel gesehen haben?
Und dennoch sagt der viel, der 'Abend' sagt,
Ein Wort, daraus Tiefsinn und Trauer rinnt
Wie schwerer Honig aus den hohlen Waben.
                                    Hugo von Hoffmannstal)

Yet there are people who know no evenings
in drastic lands where the afternoons
run on without much loss of colour
straight into absolute tunnels of darkness.
There are men who have never smoked away
a lazy hour of velvet twilight
or followed their private phantoms through
the garden paths of suggestive dusk.

There are women too who never sat
in doorways knitting their cosy dreams
from the yarn of long-legged shadows,
or by the crimson blood-light mourned
distant husbands trudging with bayonets
through foreign twilights.

                          Towards the end
of afternoons the soft brown women
of this kingdom without evenings fold
their cloths about them, stabilize the jars
upon their heads and glide between
the black banana stems – for night
reels after them along their paths.

Here where the mountains seem to tip
the darkness like a fierce effluvium
across the horn-spiked hillocks, through
the leaky huts that fill and sink,
there's no time left for mild emotions.

The wicked darkness tears with magic
fingers at the tiny slice of light
and faces tremble in the slight
intimidated flame. No time
for slow nostalgia pondering loves
that bloomed or perished in the bud.
No time for sadness, only fear.
No time to think of Spengler's cultures
rotting in the Western sun
or races growing tired and sick
and self-doubt poisoning their souls.
These men without evenings have perhaps
just enough past to make them sad,
and yet, on supping terms with terror,
they cannot contemplate decline.

Them

Show us your skyline –
No castellations (we notice) chew the clouds,
No jig-saw line of city apices
cuts a culture from the naked sky –
show us your skyline.
Shock-headed Peters of pawpaws
wipe in the wind, bananas flutter
their ragged sleeves in abandonment
permitting the glitter
occasionally
of silver-grey roofs
like upturned boats in a raucous sea.

They do not tinker with towers or raise
their windows above the short tousled trees,
they do not encounter the hawks half-way
or dominate their fields; instead
they weave the rush-mats of their low alluvial lives
ducking away beneath your seeing, beyond
your grasp. They slip for preference along

black-earth paths
smacked flat
by naked soles,
secretly sauntering
under canopies
of creaking leaves
and chunky chandeliers
of dipped bananas.

Invisible they go
through humid shadows
of the banana parishes,
serfs beneath the green
uncertain sky,
deep-rooted in the black
soft earth.
Invisible they go

towards the drums,
the permutating palms
on drunken drums,
the circulating gourds
of sick-sweet beer.
O red-eyed nights
of booze and dance,
O women's love-songs
carving the dark
like rusty bush-knives!

Them and Us

They are rooted here. Their tenuous life,
haunted by ancestors, walks beneath these leaves.
Out of sight but always well in earshot
our neighbours weave the slow grass mats
of their dark-green unfathomable lives,

whilst we in our dry, well-furnished houses
(the Protectorate served its servants well)
with house-boys polishing the spacious acres,
stare out across the smooth manorial lawns
and red platoons of cannas through the trees
to alien hills that shoulder us away.

The Conservatives

They are dreadful,
you never know for sure what drives them softly by
the bottom of the garden on their long-worn path.
At times they carry spears for a hunt
you never see,
or gourds of beer for some plantation party
you're never invited to.
They are dreadful
at going about their own kind of life
ignoring your rules –
I cannot believe that colonialism ever worked,
ever began to.
We built a wicker fence across time-honoured paths
but the paths gnawed through the fence
as it were.
We said: No cows must pass through here,
the road is for cars and members of staff,
but the herdsman's crooked spear still tops the hedges
and the cows still flow serenely down the tarmac
bearing their horns like battling standards,
still graze on fields which are building-sites now
unmoved by breeze-blocks, mixers and men.
I think they will get built into the houses:
a suitable fate for conservatives.
They are dreadful, people and cows – persisting as they do
as they are.

The Kaleidoscope

You do not know this Byaruhanga: he is short
and his belly swells like a toffee-apple above
his spindly legs, and he is black and wants
to go to school.
You would not understand the wonder quite
when one day he got a kaleidoscope and peered
gingerly down it,
if you knew nothing of his lustreless mornings
among the maize and beans, beneath
an unkempt thatch with rain
brown as tobacco juice
oozing through,
his hours of cockroach boredom.
And rare the patterns in his brain: the seasons' repetitions,
the red and black mosaics of drying coffee beans
in murram forecourts,
weave of birds in flight, of mats on floors.
So when he poked the tube against the sun
the siliceous patterns dazzled,
dazzled and danced and left him dazed
staring at us with the linings of his pockets out
for similes he does not have:
rose-windows, snow-flakes, molecules, mosaics,
a glimpse of vast complexities, of puzzling constellations,
a hint of Beauty's structures, of subtle thought
and delicate engineering.
A glimpse, no more.
Submerged keel of this racing generation,
he'll never catch the breeze, nor flutter brightly from the mast,
nor read the compass for the course.
He'll never start.

Rendez-vous

Beneath the flaming kaffirboom we used to meet, old friend,
to send our caterpillar sentences, in their own good time,
through the shadows cool.
Our lazy syllables strolled until our tongues themselves
like lazy dogs lay down on their soft palates and slept.
Flies settled on our sleeves – but we hardly felt
the need to disarrange the universe
on their account.
No minutes panted on our wrists,
I don't remember you or me being late for anything,
or early,
not having appointments to keep.
Some days we watched the sun slide down
our ropes of tobacco-smoke, our hands as still as lizards
on the cheeks of the sweet-smelling gourds,
and some days, content as we were, we even pondered some
        change,
some progress.

This post-office has advantages: it's very cool at noon
and we can talk again, our elbows on the counter
while we wait for service – the clerk is very busy
and cannot serve us yet,
but when he comes, he will have a great deal to tell us,
and being of our tribe, he will.
This post-office has advantages over the kaffirbooms,
keeps out the flies,
and while that Cambridge scholar of our village
runs to ground the yellow stamp we need,
there's time for another smoke.

Not Needed

Her mother yelped as we drew up,
and fled beneath her sheaf of herbs,
but she, the girl, unbent her back
from the shining stream,

stood straight, her breasts like little gourds,
and stared at us (pink-skinned intruders)
incuriously as if some slight
irrelevance had limped into her secret haunt.

She only had to stoop to rub
us out of mind. She stooped and filled
her bowl and set it on her head
and barefoot went.

But how her tattered skirt betrayed
the dance of buttocks going home,
and this, her way of going, was
as timeless as

her virgin posture in the stream
refuting all we were and all
of ours we thought she ought to have:
our taps and bras.

African Lovers

How often have your headlights sharp-defined
against the backwards-flowing darkness
the bowed man walking and the girl behind.

The man ablaze like a paper lantern pushes
the glare away with a defensive elbow;
his white shirt shines like a moon in the bushes.

The girl comes after like the intimate arc
of the moon's own shadow. Of course they're lovers –
although your headlights never gashed the dark

to register a furtive roadside kiss,
and only after you had turned the corner
could there have been some incidence of this.

Tandem

I have a wife, man!
See how she perches in her blue robe
behind me,
diagonal-like,
a chuckling swallow
on a telegraph wire.
Ting-a-ling!
Her little brown toes
skim the stones in the gutter,
her heart beats hard
at my back and her laughter
clutches my ears like handle-bars
against the wind.
And so we proceed like an omukama
in stately fashion
greeting our neighbours –
ting-a-ling! It's me! It's us!

Euphorbia Trees

Why cactus trees?
The hills of Toro stretch like rubber capes
humped to deflect the long green rains,

and water flows
in rapid streams or rests in convex jars
on gentle heads – no arid place

for thrifty cactus trees.

Up there, away
from all the self-defining palms and conifers,
they wave their nicked and withered arms

like some strange tribe
of grey malignant immigrants, whose stigma rattles
in the wind: beware of us.

Their leprous trunks
heave up like veteran menhirs and evolve
shockingly, as if by some

genetic twist,
not leaves and branches but the cactus limbs
which etch on golden evening skies

their patterns of disease.

Swamp

Dry-season dust-tails dogged the cars along
the orange tracks when we began to curb
the croaking swamp. Stripped schoolboys hacked
the ankles of the giant reeds. A song

rose somewhere as the rippling line advanced,
disgruntled mostly, swiping with Birmingham bush-knives
and curling sickles. Few really grasped the idea
that civilised man will not endure a swamp.

Still seeing little sense in what they did,
they burnt the grass and dug some crooked drains.
White blooms of smoke grew huge above the swamp
at dusk and exiled all the frogs' refrains.

Rough places smooth, O make! Use hand and hoe!
Control the lie of land and guide the flow
of rain. Be conquerors subduing all:
my own philosophy runs roughly so.

We cleared the thistles and the reeds, we dug
our ditches deep; then came the spearing rain.
And now the fatalists can smirk and say:
Look, sir, the grasses have grown tall again.

Trial

What happened? Who took it? Who shared the spoils?
Two prisoners sitting on stools in the porch
impassively stare, the facts buried deep
in the holes of their minds. They have spun their tales.

Bagonza has said that the other one came
with the notes in his fist. He could not refuse
the present of shillings. It was true, it was true,
as he switched on the falls of his liquid brown eyes.

Byaruhanga has told of his colleague's hand
in the drawer. Oh, he saw it all through the window.
Was that wrong? Was that wrong? His eight-year-old hands
made the helpless gestures of a maligned old man.

And Ben, who had nothing to do with the case,
who was only a friend, we prised from the wall
where he crouched with elephant ears full-spread
for the scandal a friend enjoys to relay.

Who took it? We lowered the questioning hook
into the dark and dubious waters, and fished
around the straight truth (it was latent and near)
to catch no more than a couple of probabilities.

We punished them both.

Big-Game Hunter

His house where he has honourably retired
to sip his Scotch and get his memoirs down
sprouts antlers over lintels, mounted tusks
and leopard-skins pegged out like islands on
his walls, whilst everywhere save the latrines
his patronizing boot appears on some
crushed head or prostrate corpse: the photos boast.
This ruined tenement of elephant
which blocks a tragic foreground, bursts a frame,
was never proud, autonomous and grand
but coterminous with golf and croquet: game.

His morgue of stuffed achievements dumbly brags
that Man is top-dog in evolution's chain;
all lower types must pay their humble tithes
in shape of pelts or rugs or billiard balls.
The gnarled assassin now recording his
great kills has proved, at personal risk, that lead
beats fang and claw in the hunter's hierarchy,
that Man is – to a higher power – the same.
Another theorem is that Man lets live
and leaves the game.

The Expatriate

Here I sit with every mortal gadget round me.
Klemperer conducts from his narrow groove
and Brahms breaks like a sea against the windows –
an imposing European noise.
Or, if I wish, the radio with its sorcery of wires and valves
will fill this room with tongues and tragedy.
Or when a glinting bird alights in view of these tall windows,
I snatch my violet-tinted, smooth-adjusting binoculars
to see more definitely.
These things, my adjuncts, live with me, belong these
        Siebensachen
like Jupiter's old moons to Jupiter – and yet
I'm only conscious of their modern presence when
that boy appears,
that small black boy that stands
so shyly at the window looking in
through sad soft eyes
like two dark holes
in a forest-wall.

Perfect Beggar

He squats beside an antique sewing-machine
outside the Asian store and frankly waits
for us and as we near, his face divides
like a wrinkled pod disclosing broken teeth:
an almost happy smile. And then he thrusts
the scabby knobs of leprous hands towards
your purse, as if he had some rather old
potatoes to dispose of, smiles and trusts
that you will see the meaning of his stumps:
a man who has no fingers *cannot* work,
must therefore beg. And he's content while
ten other men nearby in idle clumps
wait sour and silent, their workless fingers jammed
deep down their empty pockets.

Bakonjo

They are inferior people, ludicrously small,
uncivilised and quite beyond the pale;
when their name is uttered, we lowlanders fetch a sneer,
our children, being well-drilled, snigger and pull
rude faces at the midget stranger.

We call them, on account of their subhuman size, insects
or flies, for our fathers hunted them till they flew
into the hills and forests with their gods and history.
At night their solitary fires on the mountain-sides
recall that victory

and the need to guard our gains against the greed
and vengeance of the stunted. Yes, I warn
my people red-eyed from beer and indolence,
grown torpid under the heavy anchors of fat
bananas, their affluence

is menaced by the memories of those who, left
to clutch and scrape the vertical soil, evolved
tough thighs and nimble feet and a taste for work –
but I forget myself – an inferior people
whose children wander naked.

The Secessionists

Some men opt out of history's onward-slogging march.
Where others flow towards the lakes of nationhood
these highland people stand behind their mountain dams
indignant as the foaming streams that slap the drums
of boulders down the viper valleys to the plains.

They have an ox-bow dream, these squat, flat-footed men,
these nimble hunters of the hyrax, companions of the mists
that hug them up and down. If liberty begins
to wither in the grand republics of the plains,
frame airy constitutions in the udders of the clouds.

Tomasi, berry-bright Mukonjo, sings for us:
His people are the bees that work the mountains' shoulders;
no arm could shake them from the cells of their vertical fields.
The government sends a load of pitch-black, six-foot soldiers,
but what do they, who speak another language, know?

Tomasi in his tattered jacket sings a song
of freedom. Soft and apolitical the faces of
the little listening women. While not two miles away
the slouch-capped giants grease their guns in readiness
to implement the logic of the larger fatherland.

The Mission

For sixty years or more the mission church
has let the lantern of its chalk-white walls
so shine before the shouting mountain men
that some slight shift of soul may well
be posited.

The sabbath drums boom out their routine summons
among the candled coral trees – and down
the mountain's grassy runnels tribesmen pour
to worship and the whitewashed walls resound
with battered diatonic hymns.

The preacher preaches love: love one another.
(How can we love the plainsmen when they burn
our houses, steal our goats and rape our wives?
We'll love all men as Master Jesus did
except the lowlanders.)

On Monday morn the curling fleece of smoke
dilates above the plainsmen's huts. And down
crash axed banana trees. And leg-trussed goats
stagger and scream. Above the bedlam hangs
the white star of persistent Christ.

Political Prisoners

Efficient chap, this officer,
as he stands – a Colussus
boxed in ironed khaki,
slapping his shorts with
his shiny stick
in the prison yard.
But who are these kids
in cut-off pyjama suits?
Bakonjo.
So many?
Three hundred –
illegal assembly
and curfew-breaking –
six months.

Forlorn little men in long-sleeved vests
with wiped-off smiles
crouch like flocks of domestic birds
before the giant guards –
a legal assembly now.

They did not think the times
had changed so much,
attended weddings as before,
each taking a gourd,
and walked straight into the enemy arms
of military rule.

Poor birds,
so few were trapped in pursuance
of some ideal,
poor political gaolbirds caged
for unpolitical crimes
like being unable to read
a public decree.

So We're all Right, Mum

We had a war –
one of those tribal things,
the Bawhatsits versus Bawhosits.
It lasted several days.
(A war of several days
was long enough for many men
and many women
and many children.)

And many men
and many women
and many children
ached at the wells
of their wounds
in the wards
while their houses burned.
While their houses burned
we stood at the window and said:
They are burning the grass
at this time of year!
We also said:
They are queer.

We had had a war
it later appeared
in the capital press.
The Bawhatsits had speared
The Bawhosits some hundred yards
from our hedge and left
a number of dead.
The corpses must have been
around for days, but no–
one ever said.

Feud

After the parents have gone to burn the houses of the parents
    below
and those below in turn have burnt the houses of those above
who started the burnings,
the children of the mountains, who were hidden but saw,
are shelled by the dawn from their pod of darkness
and creep dry-eyed to the ring of homely embers
and stare at what half-charred remains there are:
a blackened stool, a cooking-pot, some tins.

And then the unhabitual silence swells all intervals,
no cocks are crowing, goats all gone.
With desolate eyes they stare across the valley
as the long sealed trains of cloud slide past
deporting their fathers and mothers. . . .

On the Great Bitter Lakes

There was a long outfaring journey once half-done
when the close shores of the Suez canal
threw back the prickling heat of a billion
polished prisms – and suddenly withdrew
leaving us steaming undefined

into a still grey lake.
The cogitating motors seemed to muse
beneath the steel: the ship moved like
a poem line for line across the silence
until it scarcely moved at all
and lay complete in anchored trance.

We hung like lifeless washing at the rail...

The ship burned white on the burnished waters
fused with its own immaculate image.
The certainties of Arabs, camels, rocks
had sunk to just a pale thin sneer
on the distant lips of the Bitter Lakes.

This place of destination seemed to be
no destination. Perhaps, from here, it was not possible
to sail straight on, with purposeful fan
unfolding aft, for ever confident
of banks and bearings.

And as we floated there detached,
softly pulsating beneath the turnspit sun
a hatch below spewed out some rotten meat
and loaves of bread that wriggled and jumped
as the fish gave uppercuts; and splintered crates
were jettisoned, and empty whisky-bottles
bobbed like drowning mariners,
and so we lingered in our rings of excrement. . . .

So now, as in the midday stillness of the Bitter Lakes,
all questions, like ill-stitched wounds,
split open again.

Vultures

Saw-edged wings cut circles of air
where the cattle die.

Eyes like gunners' buttons aim
at this strategic square.

Men wheel barrows overbubbling
with cow-intestines

from shed to shed, pausing to rest
in the vultures' sights.

Down they flop, winged appetites,
with croaking glee,

in fact no more carnivorous
than you or me.

c

A Non-Elegy in a National Game-Park

The silver tufts of grass have fed the air
with hourfuls of mealy ferine smells
and hot-backed buzzards, eagles and vultures must
have chased their murderous shadows through the bush
across the tawny dust
of nuded track
till now.

Suspended like a molten bulb of glass
on the skyline's tip, the last-fling sun
burns the raving grass to rose and gold.
Before the petrol-lamps of the southern stars
light up the creatures of the sobering park
debouch snout-first from the thorn-tree pools of shade
and start the surreptitious journeyings of night.
Give way to elephants! And being sensible you do.
You match them plod in solemn line across
the highway picking up their feet like pieces of litter
distastefully, shambling on in their overall hides
three sizes too large.

In green lagoons the sunken luggage stirs
or stands in the foot-holed mud like iron tanks
whose abject tonnage stares through tiny eyes . . .
The road runs flat through the fading park
which throws up yet the last silhouettes
of round-shouldered marabous perched like flasks
on the tray-topped prosopis trees,
yet nothing here breeds the feeling of elegy
though the world is left to darkness and
this bicyclist braving the man-eating dusk
his beer calabash on board,
who swerves in the lamps
of one last Ford.

Dry Safari

How long have I pummelled this rock-chested road?
Since I can remember. Now lips lack saliva.
In the dry I drag on my orange balloon
of worried dust. Hamitic faces
watch, a gallery of masks
enframed in clefts of grass.

I have driven to the season's shrivelled end
but the road coughs on through the tinder-dry land;
desires unechoed restate themselves like trees
yawning in the silence of the plain.
Old-necked vultures wheel ahead
with abominable designs.

This is the reckless time of the burning of grass:
necklets of fire burn deep on the darkening throat
of the escarpment; grass drops its grappling-irons of flame
on the road that runs regardless.
All this preparatory
to the planting.

But can new hopes pierce through and flower again?
The grass-fires of my crisp emotions burn
turning all to black; and slowly the fabric
of smoke drifts apart to expose
the full-moon's blood-shot eye.

Too Fragile

It must have been the chrysalids' Last Trump
for all along the sunswept forest road
rose coils of tender butterflies like gusts
of fallen petals, droves of splintered ghosts

condemned to hold up passing motorists
with fragile challenges. We too, remote
behind our wind-screen, knocked a passage through
their haunt, astonished at their fast display

of charge and countercharge, upsurge and feint,
the veering wings
vibrating with the febrile zoom of life,
and passed as merely witnesses – we thought.

But later, flat against the radiator's grill
we found the frayed white rags of short-lived wings.

Murchison

Victoria Nile, great gliding mirror, once
bearer of the perfect sky, your skin
begins to wrinkle. Your crocodiles stare thin
and cold from soupy shallows at the growing turbulence,

their ragged jaws ajar like open pliers.
Alarmed the white fish-eagles shriek above
the broken surface, shredded by stubborn rocks,
fragmented into hordes of leaping steers

tossing their horns of foam. But was there ever
the peace of the great still mirror? No doubt
the dark blind underdrifts were always at
the beck and call of the terrible windlass winding

the waters down. And so the wild waves course
along until that sickening space where
the river seems to lunge into the air
then crash as one incarnate savage force

gnawing the obdurate rocks, gouging the sand
from the bellies of the softer cliffs, and ripping
the naked roots of precarious trees with dripping
fingers, a mindless violence seeking an end

of itself in a cataclysm of pounded spray,
but always when the sun breaks free, a sort
of amending arch appears above the foam:
the counterforce of Noah's bow.

Stuck

I wonder what the hell I'm doing here
stuck fast – in my gum boots –
in almost the middle of Africa,
with the rain
slapping down on a road of tomato ketchup!

What beaming idealism was ever refracted
to such a foolish detail –
frustrated carwheels dig their graves
in rich red mud – O what
the hell –

it's all the same as trying to ban the bomb
through jumble-sales –
ideals are fine – in vacuo,
it's the imbecilities they land you in which hurt
you so.

Wildebeests

So now I've seen the massive-shouldered wildebeests
stir like wind-licked leaves on Serengeti Plains
and flee with zebras in a turbo-dust stampede.

Their flying beards, humped necks and muscle-smooth
      backsides –
I've seen this flight before: on ancient cavern walls
they dance, trot lightly, stare unblinking at the light

that chops their silent gallop through the centuries
of geologic darkness. Paleolithic fingers
rubbed in tallow-gleam the tawny colours on

the lasting surfaces. Cracked nails defined the leaping beast,
dwelt loving on the swelling shoulders, accurate
on the slender legs that bore the magic bulk of it.

Eternal images. Where axe-heads, pebble-tools or knives
evoke mere pity for those fumbling artizans,
the vision of the rugged beast on tiny hooves

marks off the man; declares the fire within the stone.

Albert Nyanza

Congolese mountains in bonnets of cloud
crocodile down the horizon, proud
by the inverting waters. The idle boats
gauge every wavelet like meter needles
swinging. Fishermen kneel on the sand
folding their nets like complex petitions,
singing all evening to limpid flutes,
and this is the hour your leopards of longing
lie down and you sit alone with your heart to draw
the glittering nets of peace ashore.

Ankole

Sussex-warm Ankole wind
brushes the glaucous hides of the hills
threadbare as schoolmasters' elbows;

posses of cowhorns grass-miles apart
bob on the slopes. No lowing leaks
through the lucid skin of wind.

There with lordly profiles stride
Bahima herdsmen, erstwhile rulers
slender in their red-hemmed waist-cloths

close behind their cattle,
far behind their times.

Fulfilment

Ibises
prod between goal-posts
with curving black proboscises,

hibiscus
flowers furl in the hedges,
the stiff side-whiskers

of the palms
flutter in the sudden breeze
and on the plantain arms

outstretched
the rain bursts like a benefice.

An Old Man Speaks . . .

I walk in Africa
with three black flies
on my shoulder,
and they're staying there
the same old size
while I get older.
I think in Africa
whether a man walks
in the sun – or dies,
he's but a spectacle
for compound eyes.

Idyll

The storm has passed, is barking its blind shins along the hills,
whilst here the grey doves rock on sorghum heads
serene in aftermath. Like brown tobacco juice
the roof-trapped water spills

from thatch on to the soft mud threshold. Cooking pots
glow dull in darkness. Light bent double at the door
shows where the children stand in awe
of your big wellingtons and knees and shorts.

You stand and summarize the damp idyllic scene.
The children stare like frightened kobs. Was this
the simple life the sour suburbans craved – the bliss
of peasanthood? If so, I wonder what they mean.

African Night

Night too black for shadows throbs like blood,
Rhythms rise from grass, transmissions cross,
crickets send their coded sequences,
percussive insects toss

their crotchets high to hang upon my ear.
Surely there is meaning? Like the calls
dashing beneath the low ionosphere
to crackling phones.

Or pathetic fallacy to twist,
are these radio messages one whit
more meaningful than all the bubblings of
this torrid night?

Co-Existence

Tread warily – the vast majorities stir
beneath your rapid sole; across your track
the rust-red, pincered, panzered columns trek
disputing right of way like barbed-wire.
Or here, like feuding Capulets, the termites heap their towers against your wattle walls,
and gnaw away your beams; so strong their wills,
your paths go *round* their multi-storied lair.
At night, as termites dash their fervent wings
against the mesh, the shrewder creeping things
slip through the door and quietly colonize,
whilst you, awake beneath your canopy,
must hear mosquitoes' warlike exercise,
and faced with sharing, learn humility.

Fish

Your smooth insinuations through the lily-stalks
have been observed; your silent promenades beneath
the skylights have ages over won you fame of grace.
They even have a simile for how you slide
through an unresisting ambience.

I see you better though, you fish-in-water fish.
You cannot hide your fighting pulse: it's all outside.
Your silken fins, those slavish fans, thresh on again
the tipping element. The engine of you strokes
and strokes to hold you down.

I see the effort to and not the congruence with;
and know that when your gills clap final lids upon
the blood and fins faint all around you at the last,
you'll roll in silence till your belly touches air
and quits your leaden universe.

Independence Anniversary

Sits like an earthy tuber
on the merry whorehouse step,
hands still as peeled-off gloves
on his open lap.

Tailored suits sway past
and patriotic skirts
like petals brush his eyes
which do not see

the freedom flags and girls;
and grips your flung-down coin
to celebrate once more
a dependence of his own.

Congolese Rebel

The world's eye focusses to take you in,
And registers the nameless numbers
Of men like you, cruel stirrings in the nerves
Of an algae-slow, green continent.
No longer savage-nude but scarecrow-style
In patterned shirt and latticed shorts,
You have, being military, a one-fifth share
In a gun – and bullets when supplied.
So your revolt depends on knife and spear:
Crude cutlery with which to carve
Acceptance for some wraith of an idea
That beats its tom-tom in your skull.

You took an oath; you swore away your life
To foreign slogans hard as clubs.
They smeared your eager limbs with magic oil
To turn you steel to Tchombe's lead.
In faith, your flimsy ambush laid, you fell
Like a leopard on the others' guns,
But they had time to shoot you once for them
And once again, on film, for us,
And what we saw beside the soldier's boot
Bore likeness to another boy.

Evening Cigarette

This evening falls across the waters
like a sigh of resignation;
me too, behind my cigarette's red asterisk,
resigned to coasting
having so far come.

The channel flows like beaten pewter,
on stricken trees the ghostly marabous
preside, whilst silently at first
three thin black slivers of canoes
inch out into the stream and turn
this way and cast against the shores
their sudden voices.

And singing they slip below the watching storks,
their paddles plucking the liquid strings;
when lake-birds rise at their approach,
impalpable the blurr of wings.
Now darkness drives nostalgia off,
I'll leave a litter of Conrad adjectives
for the wind to scatter,
dog this butt.